PETS IN THE WILD!

GOLDFISH IN THE WILD!

by Grace Hansen

Cody Koala
An Imprint of Pop!
popbooksonline.com

Hello! My name is Cody Koala

This book is filled with videos, puzzles, games, and more! Scan the QR codes* while you read, or visit the website below to make this book pop.

popbooksonline.com/goldfish

*Scanning QR codes requires a web-enabled smart device with a QR code reader app and a camera.

abdobooks.com
Published by Pop!, a division of ABDO, PO Box 398166, Minneapolis, Minnesota 55439.

Printed in the United States of America, North Mankato, Minnesota.
052024
092024

THIS BOOK CONTAINS RECYCLED MATERIALS

Cover Photo: Shutterstock Images
Interior Photos: Shutterstock Images, Getty Images, Minden Pictures, Science Source
Editor: Elizabeth Andrews
Series Designers: Laura Graphenteen; Neil Klinepier

Library of Congress Control Number: 2023947444

Publisher's Cataloging-in-Publication Data
Names: Hansen, Grace, author.
Title: Goldfish in the wild! / by Grace Hansen
Description: Minneapolis, Minnesota : Pop!, 2025 | Series: Pets in the wild! | Includes online resources and index
Identifiers: ISBN 9781098246129 (lib. bdg.) | ISBN 9781098246686 (ebook)
Subjects: LCSH: Goldfish--Juvenile literature. | Wild animals--Juvenile literature. | Wild animals as pets--Juvenile literature. | Fish--Juvenile literature. | Fishes--Behavior--Juvenile literature. | --Juvenile literature.
Classification: DDC 636.0887--dc23

Table of Contents

Chapter 1

Goldfish

Goldfish are freshwater fish. They belong to the **carp** family. They get their name for their beautiful coloring.

Watch a video here!

Goldfish are **omnivores**. In nature, they eat small animals, worms, larvae, and plants. They have teeth in the back of their throats for chewing.

Chapter 2

Goldfish in the Wild

Goldfish are found naturally in Eastern Asia. In other parts of the world, goldfish are an invasive **species**. This means that they can be harmful to other fish and wildlife.

Where Some Wild Native Goldfish Live

Long ago in China, people selected the best-looking goldfish to keep as pets. They chose to **breed** the fish that had a yellowish color. This is how the goldfish got its golden color.

Goldfish were symbols of luck and fortune in China.

Chapter 3

Pet Goldfish

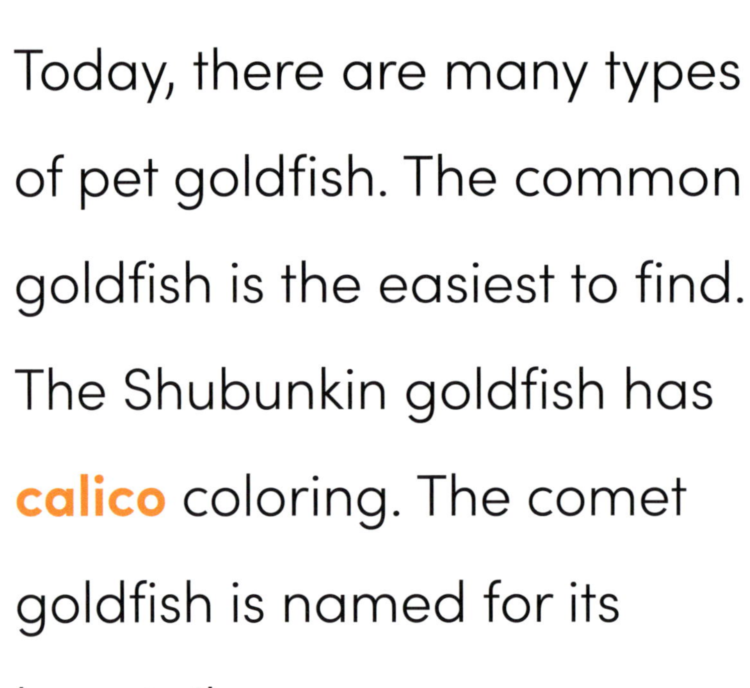

Today, there are many types of pet goldfish. The common goldfish is the easiest to find. The Shubunkin goldfish has **calico** coloring. The comet goldfish is named for its long tail.

Explore links here!

There are around 200 types of goldfish. Each one is special in its own way.

The oranda goldfish is known for its unique head. The fantail goldfish is a very popular **breed** of fancy goldfish. It is beautiful but tough.

Chapter 4

Caring for Goldfish

Pet goldfish are lively and interested in other fish. They are happy living on their own or with other fish of a similar size.

Complete an activity here!

Though goldfish are tough, they still need to be well cared for. They need an aquarium or pond to

A fishbowl is too small for goldfish.

live in. They also need clean, **aerated** water with controlled **pH** levels. Hiding spaces are also nice to have.

Pet goldfish are often fed food in flake or **pellet** form. They can also be fed live food. Healthy, happy goldfish can live 10 years or more!

Making Connections

Text-to-Self

What do you like best about goldfish?

Text-to-Text

Have you read any other books about goldfish? What did you learn in those books that was not in this one?

Text-to-World

There are many fish throughout the world. What other fish are good as pets?

Glossary

aerated – supplied with oxygen.

breed – to produce young; a particular type of animal.

calico – a color pattern that is white with black, brown, and orange patches.

carp – a large edible freshwater fish, found or bred in lakes and ponds.

omnivore – an animal that eats both plants and other animals.

pellet – a small rounded piece of food.

pH – a symbol for a measure of how acidic or basic water is.

species – animals that look alike and can have young together.

Index

Online Resources

popbooksonline.com

Thanks for reading this Cody Koala book!

This book is filled with videos, puzzles, games, and more! Scan the QR codes* while you read, or visit the website below to make this book pop.

popbooksonline.com/goldfish

*Scanning QR codes requires a web-enabled smart device with a QR code reader app and a camera.